W0081403

My Ballet Journal

Monica Wellington

—— WITH ——

Lydia Wellington

DOVER PUBLICATIONS
Garden City, New York

For our ballet mother and daughter friends:
Heidi and Sylvie, Cheryl and Shelby, Camille and Gabi.

Love, Monica and Lydia

Copyright © 2014 by Monica Wellington and Lydia Wellington
All rights reserved.

My Ballet Journal is a new work, first published by
Dover Publications in 2014.

ISBN-13: 978-0-486-78194-5
ISBN-10: 0-486-78194-1

Printed in Canada
78194108   2025
www.doverpublications.com

This journal belongs to

_____

My age

_____

My picture

My Ballet School

My ballet school: _____

Year: _____   Age: _____

My class schedule: _____

My teacher(s): _____

_____

Corrections from my teachers: _____

_____

_____

_____

My goals: _____

_____

_____

_____

Stretch taller.   More turn-out.   Reach higher.

Hold in your stomach.   Point your toes.   Don't roll in your feet.
Pull up your chest.   Straighten your legs.   Smile!

SCHOOL ANNOUNCEMENTS!

Auditions: _____

Holidays: _____

Parent Observation Day: _____

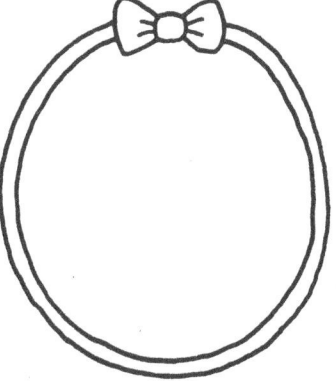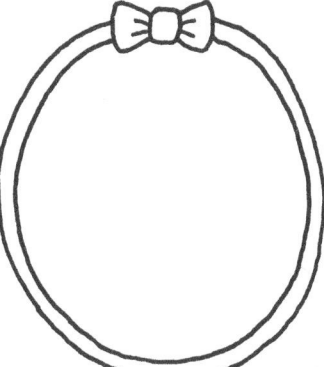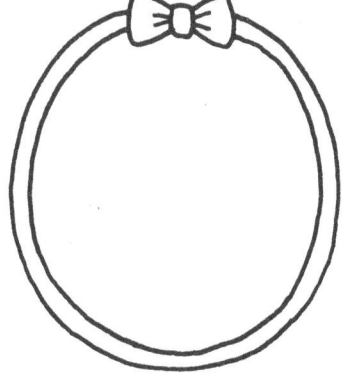

_____   _____   _____   _____

Some of my friends in my class.

(Draw their portraits or glue in their photos.)

Getting Ready for Ballet Class

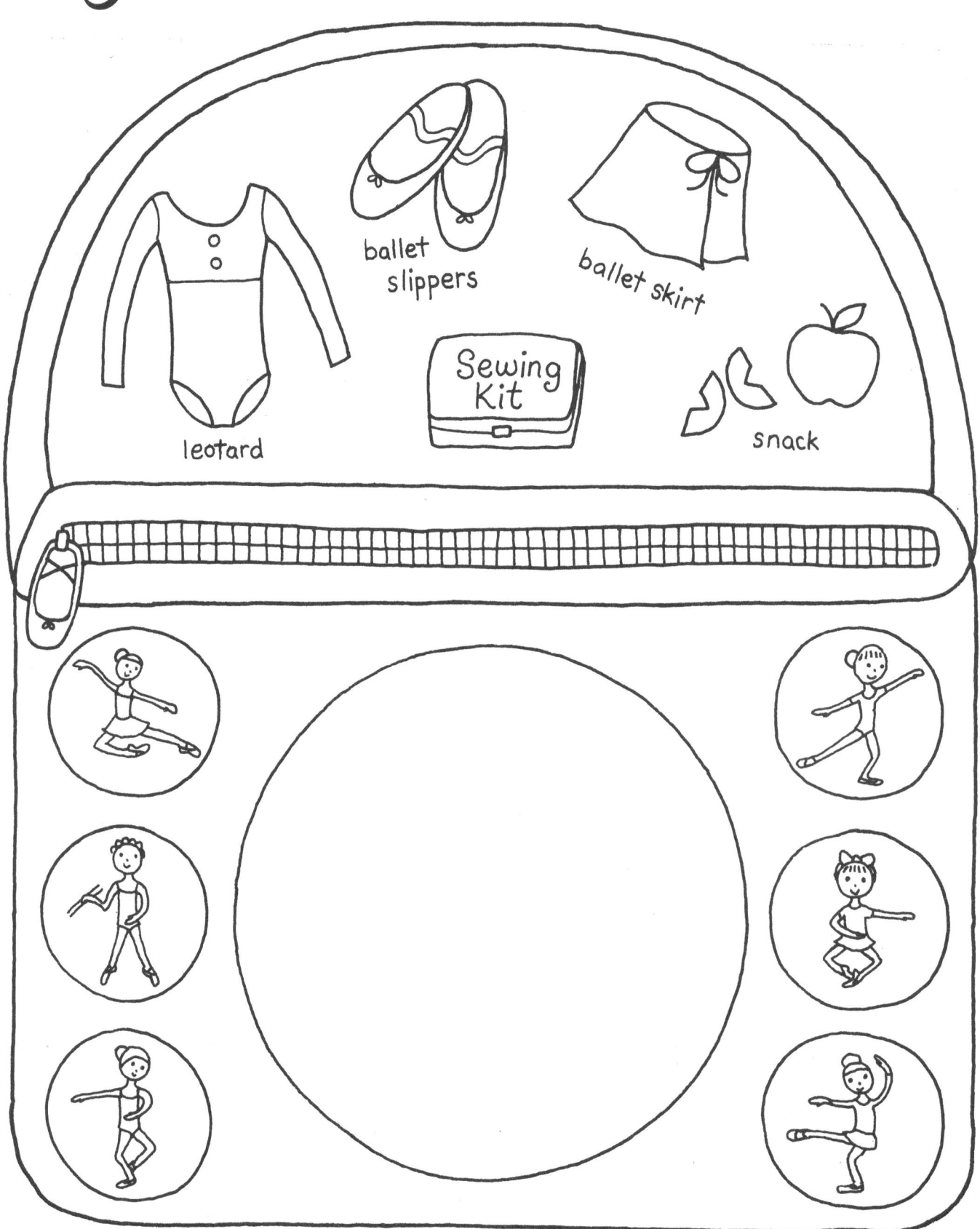

ballet slippers

ballet skirt

Sewing Kit

leotard

snack

Decorate your ballet bag.
Pack it up, and then you will be ready to go!

Checklist for My Ballet Bag

practice tutu

bandages and toe tape

thread and needle

extra leotard

scissors

makeup pouch

Remember to bring:

_____

_____

_____

_____

_____

_____

_____

pink tights

banana

heavy socks

water bottle

hairbrush and comb

hair elastics

bobby pins

scrunchie

perfume

lipstick

leg warmers

toe pads

pointe shoes

another extra leotard

small mirror

notebook and pencil for notes

Corrections from class

My Hair

My hair color: _____

My hair length: _____

For ballet class my hair must be neat and in a bun.

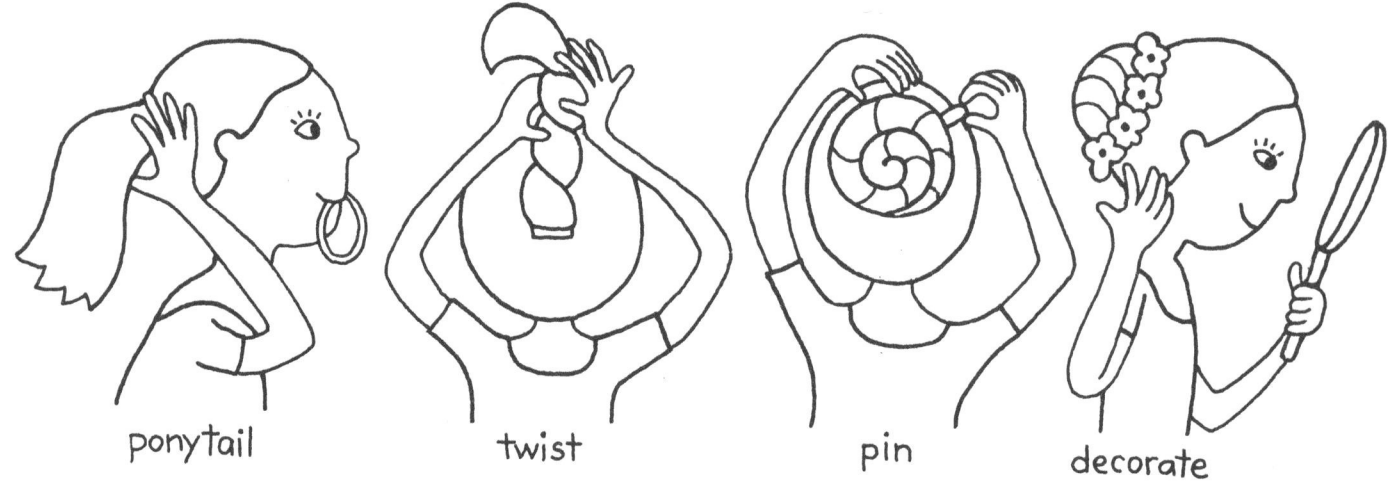

ponytail   twist   pin   decorate

For special occasions and performances I wear a sparkly, beautiful, jeweled tiara in my hair!

My Leotards

The dress code at
my ballet school:

_____

_____

Draw a picture of your
leotard for class.

I can wear different
kinds of leotards for
fun. My favorite color:

_____

Draw your favorite
fun leotard.

flutter sleeve
with miniskirt

¾ sleeve with lace

halter leotard

turtleneck
with zipper

princess seamed
with long sleeves

puff sleeve
and sequin trim

ruffle neckline
with ruffle skirt

short sleeve
empire waist

The Five Ballet Positions

first position

second position

third position

Every ballet class starts with exercises at the barre.
Here is a grand plié in first position.

When I practice these five positions in ballet class,
my teacher reminds me to: _____ Stand tall
_____

Keep my elbows lifted _____

_____

_____

_____

_____

_____

fourth position   fifth position

Other exercises I do at the barre are: _____ Tendu _____

_____ Relevé _____

_____

_____

_____

_____

Working on Correct Positions and Steps

tendu croisé devant

jeté à la seconde

frappé derrière

passé en relevé

preparation
for pirouette

turning

finishing

My corrections:

_____

_____

_____

_____

_____

_____

échappé

penché

More ballet steps I am learning:

grand pas de chat

_____

_____

_____

_____

_____

grand jeté

arabesque

bourrée

assemblé

pas de chat

développé

My Favorite Ways to Stretch

_____ _____ _____

Partnering Class

Pas de deux

Oops! Everyone makes mistakes sometimes.

My most embarrassing moment: _____

_____

_____

_____

_____

_____

I am always aiming to get better and stronger!

I am working on: _____

_____

_____

high

higher

highest

I did it:
triple pirouette!

Finally:
entrechat quatre!

keep bending:
beautiful arabesque!

My Footwear

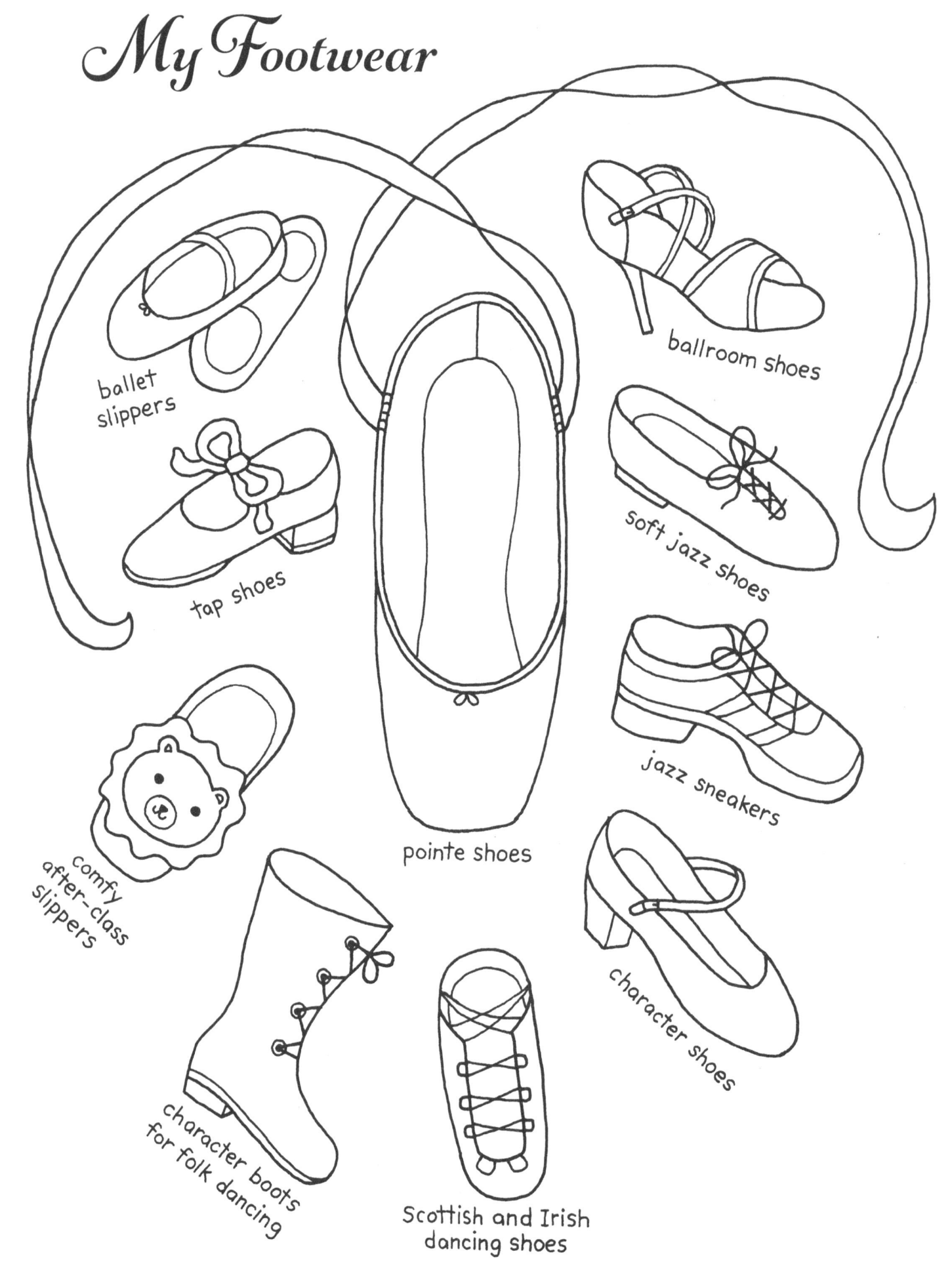

ballet slippers

tap shoes

ballroom shoes

soft jazz shoes

jazz sneakers

comfy after-class slippers

pointe shoes

character shoes

character boots for folk dancing

Scottish and Irish dancing shoes

I have these dancing shoes:

_____

_____

_____

My first pair of pointe shoes:

I was _____ years old when I got
my first pointe shoes.

Made by this company: _____

Size: _____

Specifications: _____

Hungarian dance   Scottish dance   Spanish dance

The Nutcracker

Roles I have danced: _____

_____

_____

Marie
or Clara

party guests

soldier   bunny

mouse

angel

candy cane

polichinelle

Sugarplum Fairy
with her Cavalier

Arabian

Flower

Dewdrop

Snowflake

Marzipan

When I grow up, I want to dance the role of
_____ in the Nutcracker.

My Makeup

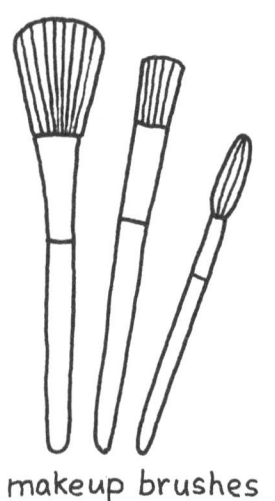

makeup brushes

When I get ready to perform on stage I carefully apply my makeup. In my makeup box I have:

powder and pad

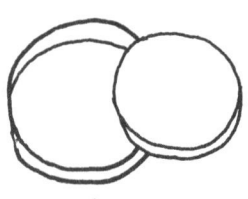

pancake and sponge

_____

_____

_____

_____

_____

_____

sharpener

sparkles

lip liners

false eyelashes

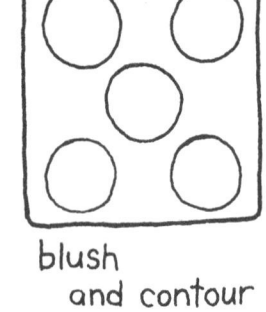

blush and contour

lipsticks

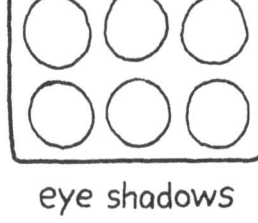

eye shadows

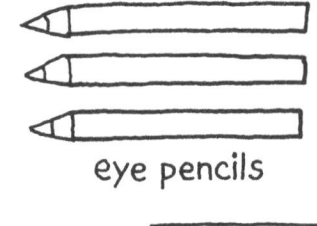

eye pencils

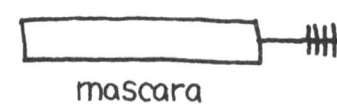

mascara

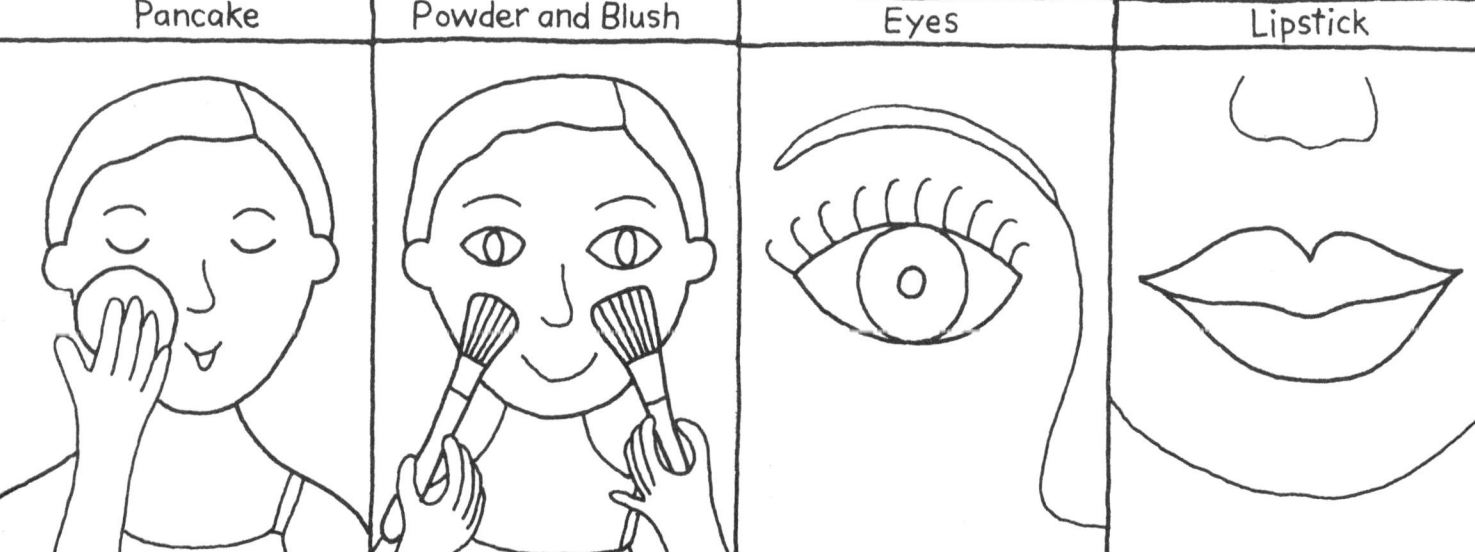

Pancake	Powder and Blush	Eyes	Lipstick

Getting ready for my favorite role!
This is me with *stage* makeup on.

Apply the makeup dramatically
so that the audience can *see*
your features sparkle
from a distance.

The Tutu

Tutus are worn by ballerinas in many famous classical ballets.

A Classical Tutu

Odette from Swan Lake

Aurora from Sleeping Beauty

Sugarplum Fairy from the Nutcracker

They are fancy and colorful with a short puffy
skirt and a close-fitting bodice. A tutu
makes you feel very elegant!

Paquita

Gamzatti from La Bayadère

Kitri from Don Quixote

You will be a ballerina too!
Design your own tutu!

My Favorite Ballets

Sleeping
Beauty

The Nutcracker

Cinderella

The Firebird

Coppélia

Swan Lake

Romeo and
Juliet

Don Quixote

Giselle

Being on Stage

My Performances

Ballet: _____

My role: _____

Date: _____

Place: _____

My costume: _____

Music: _____

Favorite moment: _____

_____

_____

Ballet: _____

My role: _____

Date: _____

Place: _____

My costume: _____

Music: _____

Favorite moment: _____

_____

_____

Ballet: _____

My role: _____

Date: _____

Place: _____

My costume: _____

Music: _____

Favorite moment: _____

_____

_____

Being in the Audience

Ballets
I Went to See

Ballet: _____

Company: _____

Date: _____

Place: _____

Dancers: _____

Favorite moment: _____

Ballet: _____

Company: _____

Date: _____

Place: _____

Dancers: _____

Favorite moment: _____

Ballet: _____

Company: _____

Date: _____

Place: _____

Dancers: _____

Favorite moment: _____

_____

Ballet: _____

Company: _____

Date: _____

Place: _____

Dancers: _____

Favorite moment: _____

_____

Ballet Dictionary

Adagio: A series of slow steps that flow smoothly.

Allégro: A series of quick and lively steps.

Arabesque: (French) A position in which the dancer balances on one leg with the other stretched straight to the back.

Assemblé: (French) A jump in which the legs come together in the air before landing in fifth position.

Attitude: (French) A position in which the dancer stands on one leg with the other bent and lifted.

Barre: The wooden rail around ballet studios that dancers hold on to for balance during class.

Bourrée: (French) Small, linked, traveling steps in fifth position on tiptoe or pointe.

Choreographer: A person who creates dances.

Composer: A person who creates music.

Corps de ballet: (French) The dancers in a ballet company who usually perform the group dances rather than the solo roles.

Croisé: (French) Crossed.

Derrière: (French) To the back.

Devant: (French) To the front.

Développé: (French) To lift the leg by sliding the foot along the other leg up to the knee before straightening it in the air.

Échappé: (French) A movement of both legs from a closed position to a spread open position.

Entrechat: (French) Crossing and uncrossing the legs in fifth position during a jump.

Fouetté: (French) Whipping the raised leg from front to side during a pirouette.

Frappé: (French) To strike one foot outward from a position curled around the opposite ankle.

Glissade: (French word) A small sliding jump that begins and ends in fifth position.

Grand: (French) Big.

Grand battement: (French) A quick kick of the leg to waist-level or higher.

Grand jeté: (French) A large traveling jump with arms and legs stretched out.

Jeté: (French) A quick tendu in which the foot leaves the floor an inch or a little jump from one leg to the other in which one foot crosses the opposite ankle in the air.

Pas de chat: (French, "step of a cat") A jump with bent knees, landing in fifth position.

Pas de deux: (French) A dance for two people.

Pas de trois: (French) A dance for three people.

Passé: (French) To balance on one leg with the other leg bent to the side and the toes pointed and touching the standing knee.

Petit: (French) Small.

Penché: (French) An arabesque leaning forward.

Pirouette: (French) Turning, spinning on one leg.

Plié: (French) A basic movement of bending the knees.

Rehearsal: A practice session to prepare for a performance.

Relevé: (French) To raise up on tiptoe.

Rond de jambe: (French) A circular movement of the leg.

Sauté: (French) A jump.

Tendu: (French, "stretched") To stand on one leg and extend the other front, side or back until the foot is pointed but still touching the floor.

Turn-out: The way a dancer's legs are rotated outward from the hips so that the knees and feet face sideways.

Note: Many French words are used in ballet because ballet originated in Europe long ago in the splendid courts of the kings, especially the French king, Louis XIV in the seventeenth century.

The End of the Year

My evaluation from
my teacher(s):

_____

_____

_____

_____

Some highlights
from my year:

_____

_____

_____

_____

My goals for next year:

_____

_____

_____

_____